IMAGES
*of England*

OLD MARKET, NEWTOWN
LAWRENCE HILL
AND MOORFIELDS

Lawrence Hill in 1939. Ducie Road is off left. In the far distance is Lawrence Hill Church, the site of the present roundabout. On the right is the Earl Russell public house. Dating from the 1860s, it was named after Lord John Russell, Liberal Prime Minister (1865-6). This part of Lawrence Hill remains intact today, including the 'K6' red telephone box which still survives adjacent to the Earl Russell. Note the prominant 'side-arms' tram poles, placed in the centre of this principal highway.

IMAGES
*of England*

# OLD MARKET, NEWTOWN
# LAWRENCE HILL
# AND MOORFIELDS

David Stephenson, Andy Jones,
David Cheesley and Ernie Haste

TEMPUS

What were you doing on 15 September 1964? This is Barrow Road: a typical Newtown scene, taken on that date. A Ford Anglia is parked on the corner of Henry Street, with Lawrence Hill off right. On the left is Regent Street, Newtown's longest. All had been demolished by 1969.

First published 2002

Copyright © David Stephenson, Andy Jones,
David Cheesley and Ernie Haste. 2002

Tempus Publishing Limited
The Mill, Brimscombe Port,
Stroud, Gloucestershire, GL5 2QG

ISBN 0 7524 2618 4

Typesetting and origination by
Tempus Publishing Limited
Printed in Great Britain by
Midway Colour Print, Wiltshire

# Contents

# Acknowledgements

The book is dedicated to Marion, Linda, Mandy and Jean.

Our thanks and gratitude go to:
David Harrison, Peter Davey, Mrs D. Pugsley, Roy Pugsley, Beryl Farrall, Harry Jones, Mary Glass, Derek Rayner, Sydney Wookey, George Gingell, Malvern Baggott, Albert Palfrey, John Boalch, Dolores Powell, Rose Harris, Betty Lewis, Margaret Harris, Edna Williams, George Harris, Beryl and Albert Carter, Steve James, Marjorie Sheppard, A.H. Leech, S. Loxton, Dorothy Tranter, Graham Tranter, the Lines family, Mr E.W. Hutton, George E. Thompson, Jill Willmott, Doreen Humphries, Lil George, Wally Webb, Mrs Nichols, Miss R. Provis, Mr and Mrs Wethers, John Merrett, Mike Tozer, Mrs Peglar and the Barton Hill History Group.

Special thanks and appreciation to:
Lyn Townsend, Wally Ball, Tony Brake, Mr J.M. Carter, Mike Baker, Jim McNeil, Dennis Stephenson, Mike Palfrey, Dennis Hutton, Pauline and Gordon Elliott, Dorothy Brown, Mike Hooper, Doreen Parsons, Noreen Shaw, William Leonard Jones, Bob Gwinnell, Harold Dancey, Ken Thomas-Courage, Archivist.
Bristol Central Library, Bristol Central Library Learning Centre, *Bristol Evening Post*.

## References:

Brown, D., *Bristol Castle and the Old Market Area*
Carter, J.M., *Investigation into the population of Old Market* – (unpublished)
Hallett, T., *Bristol's Forgotten Empire*.
Jones, A. and Brake, T., *Moorfields; Fields of Solomon*.
Stephenson, D., *History of Lawrence Hill*.
Somerville, J., C. *Thomas Soapmakers*.
Priest, G. and Cobb, P. (Ed), *The Fight for Bristol*.
Bristol Branch of the Historical Association, *Post War Bristol 1945-1965*.
*Bristol Evening Post*.
Kellys Directories.

# One

# Old Market

When the Normans under William the Conqueror built Bristol Castle, they chose the site because it was ideal for defence. At this point, the Frome (to the north) and the Avon (to the south) come together briefly before being forced apart on rising to higher ground. This made the perfect location for a castle. A ditch was dug connecting these rivers, and this forced any attacking force into a narrower and narrower approach to the castle. This is how what we now know as Old Market came into existence.

Up until around 1150, this area was known as 'the market' but some time after that, bit by bit Bristol outgrew the single market place, in common with other such towns. Others were set up to sell specialist goods by 1450. The area would now be known as The Old Market.

What were these market places like? Probably a weekly affair with rough canopies offering shelter for the traders. Later, more elaborate tents and covers were pitched in the middle of the street. Much of the market produce was brought in beyond Lawfords gate from the farms and market gardens of East Bristol.

All lands here at this time were owned by the order of St Benedict (the Church) and would stay that way until the Dissolution of the monasteries in 1535. After that date, much of the lands were sold.

Old Market was and still is a classic cigar shape, bulging to over one hundred feet wide, but narrowing down to the gates at each end. Adjacent to Jacob Street (formally Back Street) Redcross Street came into existence so that travellers could bypass the very busy Old Market Street. By 1700, most of the Old Market houses were in an advanced state of decay.

The street and the area would now turn from an agricultural-based society with small workshops and buildings into a more intensive, industrial one. It was unusual that Bristol did not follow the pattern of many of the other towns in England and build down the middle of Old Market.

Today, all the buildings have undergone some restoration and alteration, and are a mixture of adapted styles dating from within the last two hundred and fifty years.

Old Market Street was a place which was 'alive'; always brimming with people, activity and colour. It bustled with life, the hurly-burly reflecting its status as one of Bristol's historic highways and the gateway to the east of the City. Old Market was characterized by its mix of uses and its history and traditions. A part of this character stemmed from the adjacent working class areas of St Judes and St Philips. The street was a real meeting place and a hub of tram and bus routes. Vitally, it was seen as a part of Bristol's shopping zone, the natural link into the shops of Castle Street. The whole impact was heightened by the street's width and broad sweep. High profile and popular venues included the Kings Cinema, the Empire Theatre and the Methodist Central Hall. A substantial brace of pubs were part of the picture, as were a brewery and large drill hall. Behind Old Market Street to the north (Redcross Street) and south (Jacob Street) were a number of manufactories. Interspersed were the alleyways and courtyards which concealed dwellings and almshouses.

Old Market Street was the dramatic and solid link to Bristol's pre-1940 shopping centre based around Castle Street. As such it was to suffer significantly when Castle Street was firstly devastated in the Bristol Blitz and secondly, was not rebuilt by Bristol planners after the war. Old Market Street lost a vital balance, but worse was to come.

As the 1960s dawned, plans began to emerge which pointed to massive changes in the Old Market area. To relieve traffic congestion the highway engineers proposed to complete the pre-war Inner Circuit Road. This next stage would focus on Old Market. As early as 1961, the traders of Old Market were voicing their concerns as details of the sweeping proposals appeared. The plans were uncompromising in typical 1960s style; the talk was of ten-lane highways, an underpass, 'pedestrian decks' and subways, complimented by huge 'ultra modern precincts'. As the decade progressed it became clear that the Old Market works would be one of the biggest redevelopment areas in the city.

The demolition of the Empire in 1964 signaled the start of the works. However, the acquisition of sites was slow and it was not until mid-1967 that the excavators began their work on the actual underpass. East Bristolians, so familiar with Old Market Street, were soon faced by a scene described at the time as 'a no mans land of road works, centering on a massive 30 foot crater'. In October 1968 the underpass and roundabout was finally opened. The effect of the new road was to decisively cut off Old Market from the new 'central shopping area' at Broadmead. Moreover the demolition of housing to the east of West Street/Old Market also affected the character of the street. A steep decline set in, while in the background Bristol's planners considered further demolition. Gradually the mood swung behind conservation not demolition. In 1974 a combination of Bristol conservationists and the Department of the Environment successfully halted the demolition of some of Old Market's seventeenth and eighteenth century buildings on the north side.

During the 1980s Old Market, now a Conservation Area, saw a major programme of restoration and renewal. If a long way from the vibrancy of its heyday, it did reverse the sight of a mass of boarded-up properties which had blighted Old Market Street for much of the 1970s. Fortunately, Old Market Street was one of the most photographed streets in Bristol and many fine pictures remain to illustrate the vibrancy and variety of past times.

St Philip and St Jacob Church was built in 1173 by Robert Earl of Gloucester. He also built Bristol Castle. It is almost certain that there was a Benedictine Monastery on this site prior to the church in around. 900. In 1643, Captain Fiennes, in command of the Parliamentary Forces ordered the destruction of the church, but the arrival of Prince Rupert and his troops prevented this from happening. It is now known as the Pip and Jay.

Chequers public house, at No. 92 Old Market Street. On one side are the Star Coffee House, Maynards Sweets and Bryants Ropes on the corner of Tower Hill. On the other side is the former brewery, Rogers, later Simonds. The building then housed the Co-op, followed by the bus company, who used it as a canteen. The busmen used this pub as their local. It was very narrow inside, but quite lengthy. It was replaced by Castlegate, offices built in 1982/83.

Angel's Café, Old Market Street in 1965. Four doors along from the Stag and Hounds, it was demolished to make way for the underpass and roundabout. In the 1930s it was Doctors Scott and Carter's surgery.

Old Market Street in 1965. Seen here are The White Hart and the 1930s shops which survived the Blitz. On the extreme left is the turning into Lower Castle Street, where a rank of modern shops were built in the 1950s. All demolished by 1970 for the Holiday Inn Hotel. Note the Mini van, Ford Cortina Mk1 and the Thames (Ford) 400E van.

The White Hart, Old Market Street in 1965. The elaborate frontage of this pub is near the junction with Carey's Lane. It will be forever associated with the Empire Theatre (later the BBC Theatre) whose entrance was on the right. The pub was demolished in 1966, two years after the Theatre. The car passing was Ford's top of the range 1960s model, the Zodiac.

Empire Palace of Varieties. Opened in 1893 with seating for 2,500 to serve the growing suburb of east Bristol. It was built on the corner of Old Market Street and 'Captain' Carey's Lane. It had no bar, but the White Hart and the Woolpack were close by. Gracie Fields, Harry Houdini, Flanagan and Allen, Morecambe and Wise, Terry Scott plus three local lads, Cary Grant, Randolph Sutton and Dump Harris all appeared here. Closed as a theatre in 1954, it then became a BBC Television studio until it was demolished in November 1964 to make way for the Inner Circuit Road.

The Methodist Central Hall. The hall was built in 1924 on the site of an old chapel dating back to 1817. Seating 2,000, it was described at the time as 'a thriving mission to meet the needs of the people.' The Welsh miners were welcomed here in the 1930s on their way to London to protest against unemployment. The hall survived the war and the big air raid that destroyed nearby Castle Street. Slum clearances and the Inner Circuit Road sealed its fate. There were lots of proposals for its future, which were all rejected. In 1988 plans for forty-two flats were approved. The famous circular auditorium was demolished for a car park and garden.

Trinity Almshouses North, Old Market Street. Dating from 1913 and built of red brick in the Tudor style. Redcross Lane is off to the left.

The Drill Hall, Old Market. Opened on the 5 June 1915. The home of the 4th Battalion Gloucester Regiment. The two stone lions on top have long since disappeared, but the Bristol Coat of Arms bearing the words, *Virtue Et Industria* survived the Second World War. The American Army were stationed there, including at one time, world boxing champion Joe Louis. In the 1970s it was a post office sorting depot, closing in the 1990s. It now awaits to see if it has a future.

Weaver to Wearer, No.13-15 Old Market Street. On the corner of Carey's Lane; next door was the Bunch of Grapes, and Parsons the jewellers. There were hundreds of branches of Parsons throughout the country. The door with the clock above was the meeting place for lots of young courting couples. All of these buildings were demolished for the underpass and roundabout.

16th Battalion Home Guard. The winners of a inter-mobile company competition between the 9th, 10th, 11th, 12th and 16th Home Guard. One of the authors, Ernie Haste is in the centre rank, third from the left. Note that the Old Market Drill Hall was the headquarters of the 16th Battalion.

An advertisement for Weaver to Wearer.

Trams in Old Market, 1935. The tramcars loaded and unloaded in the middle of the street. A policeman is seen here on point duty at the junction with Carey's Lane. The end of the electric trams came on Good Friday, 1941 when the power cables were cut with the bombing of the Halfpenny Bridge at nearby Counterslip.

Trams in Old Market during rush hour in the 1920s. Queues of people can be seen waiting to board tramcars for Kingswood and Hanham. Horse trams began in St George in 1876. The electric tramway opened in 1895 and travelled right the way through to Kingswood. Hanham followed in 1900.

Buses in Old Market during the 1950s. Buses had replaced the pre-war trams, but there were still very few private cars. Taxi cabs stand in the middle of the road behind the underground toilets. Buildings visible include, on the left, ABC Kings Cinema, in the middle the Central Hall, and on the right the Stags and Hounds public house.

A bus at Carey's Lane. In the early 1950s, local buses for East Bristol departed from the Bristol Tramway Company offices in Carey's Lane, adjoining the Tatler Cinema. Bristol K type L3646 (HHY590) with lowbridge utility bodywork is seen here on route 236 to Broomhill Road via Barton Hill.

Peters, Brutons and Sparkes shops in Old Market Street in the early 1960s. At No. 47-48 was Peters outfitters, Brutons which sold electric gas heaters and Sparkes, gown specialists. These last two shops were demolished in 1966 to widen the Old Market Street/Lawford Street junction.

The Masons Arms, No. 53 Old Market. Dated 1630 it has a rendered timber frame, brick-side gable stacks and a cross gabled pantile roof, three storeys, an attic and a basement. The shop front and plate glass sash windows are nineteenth-century additions.

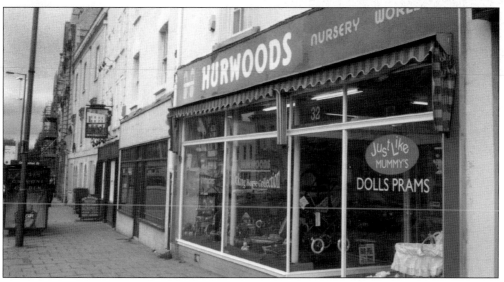

Hurwoods. I wonder how many Bristol mothers bought their babies prams in Hurwoods at No. 32 Old Market Street? However, how many people knew that Walter Charles Hurwood started business in 1899 as a sewing machine agent after moving to Bristol from London? In 1912 he opened a shop at No. 32 Old Market Street. By 1926 Mr Hurwood was selling baby carriages and toys. In 1983, the business was purchased by Mr and Mrs Hurst who have kept the Hurwoods name and expanded the business.

At No. 46 Old Market Street was H.A. Raselle Ltd, a well-known Bristol pawnbroker's shop. The traditional sign of the three balls used to hang outside the shop. According to the sign in the window they had been in occupation for 188 years. By 1984 when this photograph was taken it was the last surviving pawnbroker's shop in Bristol. In 1944 there had been eighteen.

Number 120 Jacob Street (formally Back Street). These buildings are still intact today. Everything else in Jacob Street has long gone, including the old Rogers brewery. J. Lenton & Son had been sheet metal specialists since 1881.

Kings Cinema, Old Market Street. Built in 1911, it seated 1,345 people. In 1920 it was taken over by the ABC group. Major surgery would change the Kings beyond recognition. After fire destroyed it on 20 March 1926 it was again rebuilt, altered and extended. The following year saw the twelve piece Kings Symphony Orchestra play there twice a day. In March 1929 it became the first cinema in Bristol to be wired for 'talkies', for Al Jolson's *The Singing Fool*. It ended its days in December 1976 showing X-rated soft pornographic films.

Old Market Street in 1966 before the roundabout and underpass transformed the view. Looking towards Castle Street, Carey's Lane is off to the right. In the centre are the Old Market toilets. These were underground, with glass panels set in the pavement to admit light. The same design was to be seen on the Welsh Back/Bristol Bridge junction and in front of the Bay Horse inn. The Old Market toilets were removed in 1966 in preparation for the roundabout. They were filled in and are probably still there, or at least the walls are.

The Old Soap Works, now Gardiners. Christopher Thomas (Born in 1807) took over a soap and candle works owned by the Fripp family (1783-1856). He introduced many workers perks long before other firms, including pensions, doctors visits, holidays and outings for the staff. He was also a local councillor and Justice of the Peace. He died in 1894 and in 1913 the firm was taken over by Levers, which later became Unilever. They closed the business in 1954 with a loss of 355 jobs and the premises were sold to Gardiners, Rediffusion and Hardware Ltd.

Temple Way in 1966, looking towards Old Market Street. All was to change for the underpass and roundabout. The modern *Evening Post* building was built to the right of the photograph between 1970 and 1974. Temple Way has been progressively widened and altered over the last thirty-five years, and today bears no resemblance to how it looked in 1966.

Barstaple House (South Trinity Hospital). A picturesque set of almshouses on the corner of Old Market Street and Midland Road, founded by John Barstaple, a wealthy Bristol merchant in the fourteenth century. The original almshouses were demolished in the 1850s. Between 1857 and 1858 the majority of the present Tudor-style buildings were erected. The almshouses are set around a neat courtyard with spiral stairs and timber balconies.

Barstaple House. Seen here is the west wing from Jacob Street, with Old Market Street off to the left.

The Rose and Crown Inn at No. 9 Redcross Street. Mentioned in 1775, this pub was next door to the Tatler cinema on the corner of Carey's Lane. Together with the Bunch of Grapes and the White Hart, it was one of the Courage pubs which were pulled down for the underpass and roundabout. Redcross Street, running parallel with Old Market Street, was originally a medieval lane taking traffic on market days.

Old Market Street, 1986. The northern side, having been in a very poor state throughout the 1970s, was restored in the 1980s. There were two pubs in the street called the Bunch of Grapes. One was pulled down for the roundabout and the other was merged with the adjoining café and became the Old Market Tavern.

Old Market, 1967. Excavations for the underpass: 'The Big Hole'. A few months earlier this had been Carey's Lane. Work started on the underpass in the summer of 1967 and soon a huge crater straddled Old Market Street and Temple Way. Reports at the time highlighted the pedestrian chaos and the effect on the traders of the area. Note the Stag and Hounds pub in the background.

The Prince of Wales public house at No. 8 Tower Hill, on the corner of Jacob Street. It was once owned by Simonds Brewery. In 1946, Lily Dark was the landlady, and she stayed until 1952. The building was demolished in 1980 for the building of the Castle Gate offices.

Kingsley Hall at No. 59 Old Market Street. A brick-clad, timber-framed building over three floors with limestone dressings, built in 1706 and restored in the late nineteenth century. The ground floor is set back beneath the overhanging upper storeys and supported by five columns with flared capitals and cast pedestals. It was used for many political and trade union meetings in the past, and is now offices.

# Two
# West Street/Midland Road

West Street was the key eastern approach to the Lawford's Gate, Old Market Street and the city. In medieval times this was a basic dirt track which saw the bustle of traffic heading for the old market and the passage of travellers to and from Gloucestershire. During the Civil War the area was part of the eastern defences of the city.

At the point at which West Street joined Old Market Street stood the Lawford's Gate. It was built around 1373 when Bristol received its Royal Charter and acquired lands to the east formerly in Gloucestershire. Lawford's Gate was to play an important part in Bristol's history as it was the major gateway to the city and welcomed Henry VII, Elizabeth I, Charles I, Charles II and Oliver Cromwell. This very busy arched structure was repaired in 1721, but by 1769 had become a serious obstacle to the traffic of the time. Reports highlighted that carts often got stuck in the middle of the gateway! Together with adjoining houses it was demolished to widen the approach into Old Market.

During the sixteenth and seventeenth centuries, West Street saw the building of traditional timber-framed houses and shops. This reflected the increase in population and the drift of building expansion eastwards. These early Tudor and Stuart structures were largely replaced by a range of eighteenth and nineteenth-century properties, many of which remain in West Street today.

Adjoining West Street and near the Lamb Inn was Gloucester Lane. This was an important thoroughfare in the eighteenth century. The Lane's Plume of Feathers tavern was popular with travellers arriving to Bristol from Gloucester. By the mid-Victorian period Gloucester Lane had acquired a notorious reputation based upon its drinking establishments, lodging houses and brothels.

By 1900, West Street was a key part of Bristol's eastern urban shopping line: the 'golden miles' of shops which stretched from Castle Street to St George. Through most of the twentieth century, West Street had a distinct character and for many years had a 'high street' feel – a good example of this being that in 1965 West Street could boast four banks. There were also butchers, drapers, house furnishers, outfitters and an indoor market, to name just a selection of the retail outlets. It was a real 'community' road, serving the people who lived nearby.

During the 1960s, the character of West Street was deeply altered. Central to this was the changing environment. The surrounding streets were affected by major redevelopment, with clearance and demolition resulting in a sharp decline in the population. Then, post-1966, West Street became a one-way 'traffic corridor', a place to speed through on the way to town. Many traders and the banks left and the Trinity Street corner (including Stocks jewellers) was pulled down. Like Old Market Street, West Street became isolated and rather anonymous. Still, the buildings, some of them listed as being of historic or architectural interest, remain to give clues to past times.

The Palace Hotel, Old Market. The Palace Hotel is better known locally as 'The Gin Palace' and was built in 1869. It was intended to be part of a larger railway hotel but was never built as the Midland Railway moved to a joint station with the Great Western at Temple Meads. This pub is also famous for its sloping floor and was featured in the 1962 film *Some People* which was made in Bristol. Harry H. Corbett (of *Steptoe and Son* fame) was filmed inside for one of the scenes.

Wesley Chapel Parade from Barrow Road, Newtown, passing through West Street towards Old Market. The policeman pictured is controlling the traffic at the junction with Lawford Street and Midland Road. In the foreground is a police control box. Painted in dark blue livery, inside was a telephone. When the top light flashed the constable knew that he was wanted. This was in the early 1950s. It would be many more years before the police had two-way radios.

Rowcliffes workers. This line up of workers are from T.H. Rowcliffe and Sons Ltd, makers of boxes and packing cases. Their workshops were situated between Waterloo Road and West Street. The men are standing outside the West Street entrance. In the background is Gloucester Lane with the shop belonging to Clarke and Company, gown specialists, on the right-hand corner.

Number 27 West Street. On the corner of Gloucester Lane, the two buildings on the right have now been demolished, and the window graphics have been renovated. The former bank with the words, 'St Philips Branch' still above its door is now a nightclub.

Numbers 38-42 West Street. No. 38, owned by Kenneth Harris, had been a florist for many years. The takeaway had been a laundry back in the 1950s. No. 42, the meat traders company had formally been a hide market.

The West of England Meat Company. West Street and Old Market Street were once Bristol's main centre for the wholesale meat trade. Men wearing white coats could always be seen unloading and loading carcasses. The West of England Meat Company was situated at West Street. The workforce are pictured standing proudly outside the shop. The bicycle illustrates how local deliveries were made in the 1920s and 1930s.

The Jolly Nailers – 82 and 84 West Street. This is an eighteenth century building which still exists, although it closed as a pub in the late 1950s. A George's pub, Alfred Rogers was the landlord in 1953.

The Rising Sun Inn shows impressive pub architecture at No. 68 West Street. A George's house, Bernard Callaway was the landlord in the 1950s. The building is now a windsurfers shop. The telephone box has long since gone but the pavement vent remains.

Gloucester Lane show yard – one of the West Country's oldest fairground firms, Anderton and Rowlands, had a yard at Gloucester Lane. During the Second World War, fairs were held in the yard, often frequented by American GI's who were billeted in the nearby Drill Hall. Anderton and Rowlands travel all over the West Country during the summer months and now winter in Plymouth and Collumpton.

Gloucester Lane show yard. Each October, lorries and caravans would cram into this small yard. The showmen spent the winter months repairing and painting their equipment before the season started again in March. On cold winter nights the warm glow from the caravans was a welcome sight when passing the yard. The yard is now only used for the storage of old lorries.

West Street pictured in Edwardian days, looking towards Clarence Road. Today most of the buildings remain in place but the volume of traffic is somewhat greater!

B.C. Shepherds Ltd, at Nos. 36-52 Clarence Road and Nos. 77-83 West Street. A very high-profile East Bristol department store, the business began in 1880 and in its prime employed over one hundred people. Staff included two floor-walkers to guide customers to the right counter. Miss Shepherd took over from her father Benjamin and with other directors ran the firm. Clothes, dress-material, china, household goods, bedding and haberdashery were all sold. Money was passed to the cashier via a rail system. The shop was bombed and destroyed in November 1940. They moved the short distance to 77-83 West Street. Although in smaller premises, Shepherds remained a respected and popular store for people in the area. It closed in October 1965.

34

The Greyhound Inn, 1956. Located at 17 Midland Road, it was a Bristol United Breweries house. Next door on the left, is Ernest Parlour's butchers shop. Off right, Miss R Jones' sweet shop.

Old Humphrey, No. 13 Midland Road. This business was run by Mrs E.L. Goldstone from 1930 until 1948. This building dates from around 1908. Built in the gardens of cottages which still stood for a while behind the shops. In 2001 a forty foot well was discovered in the basement. The Greyhound Inn (No. 17) stood near by.

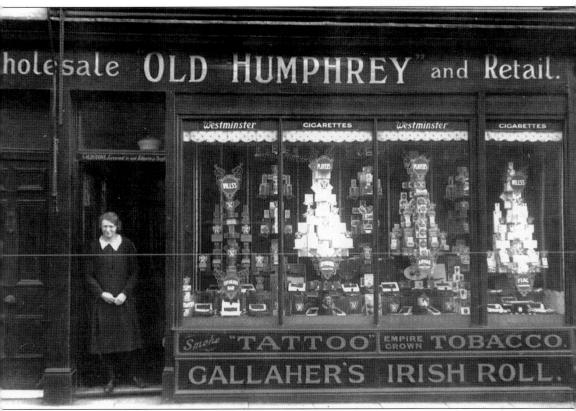

On the corner of Midland Road and Waterloo Road, stands the Swan public house. This row of shops were built in 1909 to replace a row of old cottages. Two doors from the Swan can be seen Midland Road Post Office and in the extreme background the Palace Hotel. The landlord of the Swan in 1944 was Fred Feltham.

The Midland Inn was built around 1860, at No. 14 Midland Road. Midland Road was formally known as Whipping Cat Hill, so named after a whipping post which stood nearby. Unity Chapel stood on one side of the pub and Willway Street on the other. Gardiner Haskins bought the property and demolished it in October 1998. Why did they do it?

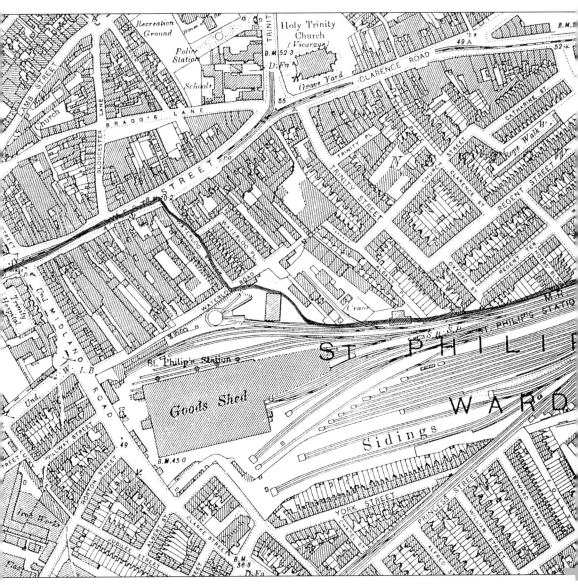

This 1906 map shows the presence of the Midland Railway. Although the passenger station was small, the goods shed was an impressive structure. Unfortunately it was destroyed by German incendiary bombs on the night of the first Bristol Blitz.

A view from Barrow Road Bridge on 30 May 1922 showing the vast expanse of the Midland Railway goods yard at St Philips. These were the days when most long distance goods travelled by rail. The signal box at Barrow Lane controlled movement of trains to and from Avonside Wharf, St Philips Goods Yard and St Philips Station. By 1967 the station had gone, the goods

yard had closed and only the Avonside line remained. The signal box was therefore made redundant. One Sunday morning, two British Railway workers arrived with sledge hammers and smashed the signal box to smithereens. Everything in the box including all its equipment was destroyed. A prime example of Corporate vandalism.

St Philips Station. The station was opened by Midland Railway on 2 May 1870. Trains ran to Bath Green Park, with connections onto Bournemouth over the Somerset and Dorset Joint Railway. The station was wooden with only one platform. In British Railways days, former LMS 2-6-2T No. 41249 is seen departing with a local train to Bath Green Park. In the background can be seen the three storey goods offices, Unity Chapel (demolished January 2002) and Waterloo Garage. The station was closed on 21 September 1953.

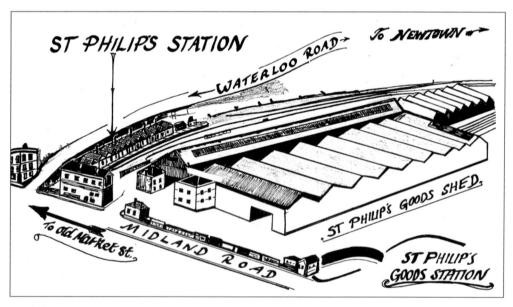

St Philips goods and passenger stations. The drawing illustrates the layout of the site in the 1930s. Note that the actual passenger station occupied only a small part of the extensive site. The goods station was dominated by the large shed which boasted elaborate facilities for the handling of goods. This structure was badly damaged in the Bristol Blitz, its distinctive multi-span roof being destroyed. The shed was not rebuilt and after the war, the 'roads' were largely open to the elements. On 1 April 1967 the goods yard finally closed. Clear evidence of the depot remained until 1975 when St Philips Road and industrial units were built on the site.

# Three

# Clarence Road

Unlike West Street, Clarence Road today looks completely different from the road as it was before the 1970s. Although a relatively short stretch, Clarence Road was particularly interesting and significant, linking Lawrence Hill and Easton Road with West Street/Old Market. Part of the ancient 'London Waye', in the seventeenth, eighteenth and nineteenth centuries buildings were erected. In the 1830s it became known as Clarence Road, after the Duke of Clarence. The development of Newtown to the south was instrumental in creating the road's vibrant blend of shops which served the growing community.

Despite suffering significant damage during the Blitz of 1940/41, a 'snapshot' of the Road in the 1950s would reveal a varied assortment of traders. These included the spartan Clarks pie shop, Lewis's umbrella shop, J.H. Mills the grocer and the Co-op hardware store on the corner of Trinity Street. The fondly-remembered Peacocks departmental store was a focal point, while the Blackmoors Head and the Red Lion were pubs of character and history. Like West Street and Lawrence Hill, Clarence Road had an intriguing mix of shop fronts, advertisements and 'street furniture'.

As the 1960s progressed it became increasingly clear that the fate of Clarence Road would be linked with the huge redevelopment of Lawrence Hill and Newtown. Big changes finally came in 1970/71 when the remaining shops on the Newtown side of Clarence Road were pulled down. On the opposite Holy Trinity Church side, the process of dereliction and demolition would take a further eighteen years.

A significant loss was the Red Lion Inn, which had stood near the junction with Easton Road. The survival of this pub would have helped to balance the harshness of the redevelopment, and pub retention was an approach adopted in Barton Hill and St Judes. However, no Newtown pubs were thought worthy of saving. The site of the pub eventually became the site of some 'greenery'. The planners even decided to place a bench seat on the site. In 1978/79 two extra traffic lanes were cut on the Newtown side, so creating a dual-carriageway to ease traffic congestion from Lawrence Hill roundabout. Ten years later the last three empty buildings of the old Clarence Road were pulled down. The demolition of these old shops signaled the final demise of the Clarence Road which many people remembered. Its replacement, despite the greenery, is just a soulless dual carriageway.

Lawford Gate Prison, Trinity Road. The 1831 riots in Bristol saw this prison set ablaze and the prisoners released. The prison was opened in 1791 on the site of a much smaller one. It contained forty cells for men and women, measuring 7ft 4in x 6ft 1in. Inside each was a cast iron bedstead, straw mattress, blanket, sheet and a double rue. There was also a chapel and an infirmary. The prison was disused by 1860 but the court and petty assizes were still used into the 1890s. It was demolished in 1907 and the present park was created (Trinity Road).

The old police station, Trinity Road. In 1836 Bristol's police force began operations and one of the station-houses was at St Philips near Holy Trinity Church. This picture shows the station, opened in 1869 in Trinity Road. It was eventually replaced by the current police station, opened in February 1979.

A charabanc at Trinity Church, about to depart on a women's outing, c. 1913. The charabanc was probably owned by the Morning Star Company, who's garage was situated around the corner at No. 55 Lawrence Hill.

Hannah More Church of England School, Trinity Road, near Bragg's Lane. Hannah More (1745-1833) was a noted playwright, school pioneer and Evangelical Christian. In her will, she left a sum of monies to Holy Trinity Church. As a consequence, the school buildings opposite the church were erected in 1838/9. In the 1950s, the school consisted of junior, mixed and infants classes, before moving to New Kingsley Road in the 1960s. To the left of the school building was the site of Bristol's first branch library in 1876. Today the whole site is occupied by the Trinity Road Police Station.

A class at Hannah More School. The infants were mixed but the older classes were separated into girls and boys. The school had close ties with the church and harvest time saw pupils take fruit and vegetables over to Holy Trinity.

Holy Trinity Church, an elegant and spacious Anglican church built by Rickman and Hutchinson between 1829 and 1832. Constructed with Bath stone in the Gothic style. This view looks towards the west front and its graceful and unusual pair of octagonal towers. The Revds Claxton and Barff were high-profile vicars in the 1940s and 1950s. By the late 1960s, numbers attending had fallen sharply and the church was finally declared redundant in 1977. The building has been used since as a community centre.

The interior of Holy Trinity Church. The church could seat 2,200, 1,500 of these being free. The word 'free' was printed on the side. In 1882 extensive renovations were undertaken. Dry rot had effected the whole of the ground floor, windows were replaced and new lighting installed. The photograph shows the wedding of Margaret Lewis and John Harris on 29 September 1973. Margaret was the daughter of Reg and Betty Lewis of Clarence Road. (see umbrella shop)

Rose Harris, florist. Rose opened this shop in 1931 selling flowers, fruit and vegetables. Starting up with only £5, she bought all her produce from the local market-gardeners of East Bristol. She was told that the shop originally had a date plaque attached, from around the 1600s. Her husband was known as Packo Harris, (a family nickname, as he was always hungry). The shop was condemned with the rest of Clarence Road and was demolished in April 1971. Workman who went down into the cellars said it was only the other two shops that held this one up! Rose also had another shop in Two Mile Hill.

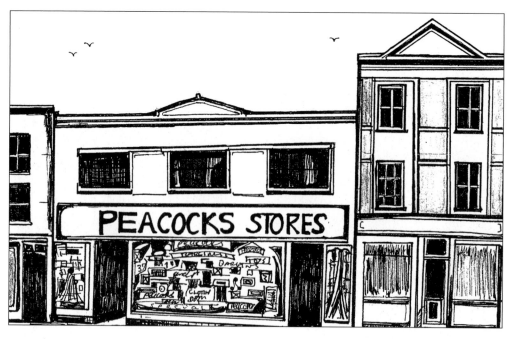

Peacocks. A popular departmental store, selling a multitude of different items, which opened in Clarence Road around 1911. Originally known as Peacocks Bazaar, by the 1950s the wording 'Peacocks Stores' adorned its distinctive façade. The store closed in 1965, the building becoming a bingo and social club. The increasingly isolated structure was demolished in the early 1980s, and was replaced by a particularly unattractive office block.

Lewis Bros at No. 49 Clarence Road, sports outfitters and umbrella makers. Reg Lewis and his wife Betty took over the shop in 1935 in the days when umbrellas were repaired rather than replaced. They collected them from most of the major stores – Austin Reed, Dunn's and Lewis's – once a week, to repair them at their shop. In 1973 the telephone exchange purchased the shop. It was finally demolished in 1989.

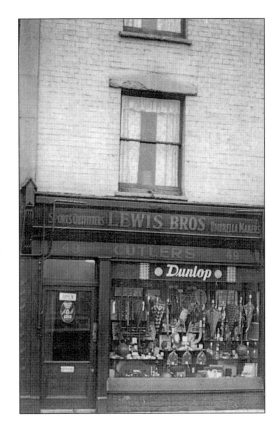

Reg Lewis in the shop.

The Red Lion Hotel, Nos. 65-63 Clarence Road, near the junction with Easton Road. A neat and stylish example of public house architecture, it was mentioned in the 1794 Bristol Directory. In 1956 Mrs Mary Ashdown was the landlady, but by July 1972 its days were numbered. A regrettable demolition.

Outside the Red Lion Hotel. This ladies coach party poses in Clarence Road before a trip to London, c. 1946.

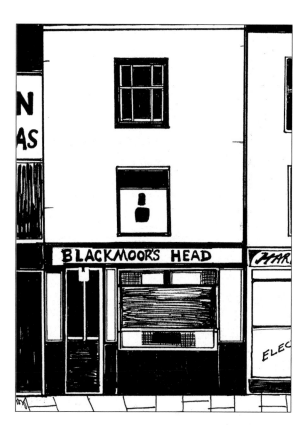

The Blackmoor's Head, No. 55 Clarence Road. A pub which very probably dated from the seventeenth century if not earlier, it was included in a 1793 guide to Bristol. It was situated near an ancient lane which stretched through Easton. In the late 1950s the pub closed, and the building became part of the adjoining electrical shop.

Clarence Road looking towards West Street. Note that there are no cars on the road, only one horse and cart, a bicycle and a tram. Shepherd's, off left, had all the shops from Nos. 36-52. A very busy street, children on the right of the image stand and watch the camera.

Clarence Road in 1968. The Peacocks building is pictured, centre left. Demolition had not yet begun, and the intimate street scene can still be appreciated. In the distance looms the brand new Croydon House tower block – a sign of the new landscape. The buildings on the right had been cleared by the end of 1971. A wide grass strip and then the present dual carriageway totally transformed this scene.

The last three shops to survive on Clarence Road. By the mid-1980s the demolition was almost complete; No. 49 Clarence Road was boarded-up already. This shop was formerly Lewis's. Number 51 Clarence Road was the opthalmic opticians and No. 53 Clarence Road was Milsom's, a fresh fruit and vegetable mini-market. All three properties were demolished shortly after the photograph was taken in July 1989.

The General Store at No. 9 Easton Road was owned by the Lines family. They also owned a taxi-cab business at No. 30 Easton Road, and another on Lawrence Hill. The Lord Chancellor public house was next door at No. 7.

The tobacconist at No. 11 Easton Road – another Lines family business, selling tobacco, sweets and newspapers. No. 13 was the local fish and chip shop, followed by the Paddock and Thrissell Street.

Easton Road. This picture taken in 1986 shows numbers 9, 11 and 13 Easton Road awaiting demolition. The old Thrissell building, with later owner Langston's name on the wall, is on the corner of the Paddock (see map).

Easton Road from Clarence Road. The demolition of numbers 9, 11 and 13 Easton Road and the Thrissell Engineering Company works, in December 1988. Thrissell's were designers and manufacturers of specialist machinery for industrial firms and were founded in 1805. Note the 1930s 'K6' red telephone box which was removed shortly after this picture was taken.

Easton Road in 1988 during the demolition of Thrissell's. The image was taken looking from Easton Road into Thrissell Street. A business park was built on the site in 1989. In the 1970s the firm was known as Mason Scott Thrissell and considerably extended the Easton Road/Stapleton Road works.

Thrissell Engineering Stores. The Thrissell Engineering Company stores office staff pose for the camera in 1945. A lady can be seen here demonstrating the elaborate card system used to find parts. Another lady is on the telephone while the foreman looks on.

Thrissell's Nomads, 1963. The team played Bristol City in the junior cup in 1963. The Nomads won 2-1. They also won the Bosley cup and League cup that year. The lucky mascot was Ian Elliott.

Wessex Coach Station. Believe it or not, this overgrown bomb site was used by Wessex Coaches in the 1950s and '60s as a coach station. The buildings were destroyed during the Bristol Blitz. The entrance to the site was through a doorway next to the Bunch of Grapes public house at Clarence Road.

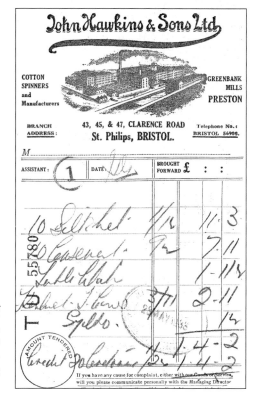

John Hawkins & Sons Ltd, 1933. The days of firms issuing receipts like this – priced per item, and brought forward have long gone. Hawkins occupied a fairly elaborate building at Nos. 43-47 Clarence Road. They sold items made at their Preston factory.

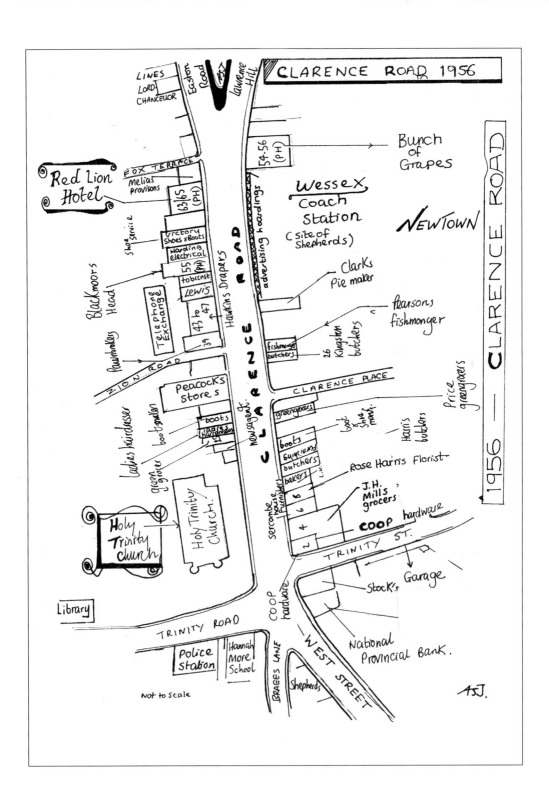

A Map of Clarence Road as it was in 1956.

56

*Four*

# Newtown Remembered

## by Lyn Townsend (née Lynda Dickens)

'Until I was about ten years old, I lived at number 6 Church Street, Newtown. It was my grandparents house and, as was usual then, my parents lived with their parents. My grandfather was a huge tall man with rolled-up shirt sleeves and braces. He used to sit in the armchair, cleaning out the turn-ups in his trousers. Because both my parents were short – dad was 5ft 4in and mum 4ft10in, my grandfather seemed like a giant. My grandmother died before I was born. Mother was a dressmaker, a job she could do from home as she'd had to take care of a mother crippled and bedridden with arthritis. She would take me with her to buy fabric in Shepherds, a huge shop in West Street, which had bare floor boards, thin round-backed chairs for customers to sit on and a pipe system in which the money was put in a little container – it whizzed off across the room to a woman sat in a little box, then came back with receipt and change.

We would walk to the Christmas Steps to buy buttons and trimmings in Trulls. My dad was a French polisher by trade but with when there was no work in polishing he took many jobs – milkman, paper man, labourer at the St Anne's Board Mills, and he worked nights making wooden toys in Cheltenham Road. My mum worked nights counting card at the Board Mills too, and my granddad would look after me if they both had to work. The Christmas parties at the Board Mills were terrific; we would wear Davey Crockett hats, play games, receive a Christmas present from Father Christmas and have a great time.

We lived in a 'doorstep' terraced house with no barton, front garden or bay window – just flat-fronted, directly onto the pavement. We had a front 'best' room and back 'living' room, and were one of the first families in the street to have a bathroom built on. The stairs were in two parts with a big skylight in the ceiling above. The 'V' of the roof went through the middle of the house but because of a false façade, from outside the roof looked flat. Everyone left their front doors open and we had an inner door with half stained-glass. If someone called they would open the inner door and call out.

Because I was a very 'cross' child, my mum would let me play in the coal hole under the stairs – anything for a bit of quiet. The third bedroom was entered by going through the back bedroom, but it was never occupied as it was damp and I was sure, haunted. I slept in the front bedroom in a bed along side my mum and dad's bed, as I suffered from nightmares and had to hold my mum's hand across the space between the beds until I fell asleep (which was probably why I had no more brothers or sisters). Our garden was very long and thin, about a hundred feet long which backed onto small gardens of the houses behind in Regent Street. I had a swing at the bottom which my dad made out of pieces of wood and string which would frequently break, and I would end up on the concrete path.

We lived in the middle of a street with two pubs, The Dove on the opposite corner and the Foresters Arms on our corner. The lady that used to run the latter was a short, plump, Spanish looking lady with her hair pulled back into a bun, always wore black and had a young daughter. The Dove's owners had two sons, and a daughter, I think.

On the other side of the road to our house was a very tall wall of a builders yard (as tall as our house). The girls from our street used to play ball and practice handstands against it. We would double-skip with two skipping ropes across the street and see how many of us could skip together. There were always lots of children to play with of all ages as most families had four or five children. We used to play outside our house in the road as by evenings there wasn't any traffic as hardly anyone had cars. We would play games such as 'What's the time Mr Wolf?' where one child used to stand face towards the wall, and the rest of us would creep up behind stopping stock-still at one o'clock, two etc. If we should be caught moving or wobbling we would be 'out'. Other favourites were 'Statues' and 'Hide and Seek'. I used to make dolls clothes from mums scraps of material at Patricia Caine's house in Clarence Parade.

The boys used to hang string from the arm of the converted gas light outside our house to make a swing and I would be tied to the lamp post when we would play Cowboys and Indians.

The first house past the wall of the builders yard was a converted shop in which a large family lived, I think all girls. My mum used to make lovely bread pudding, and I remember bartering with one of the girls for a large piece of bread pudding in exchange for a Post Office set, which my mum would never let me have.

At the end of the street was a bomb-site (Wessex Coach Park) which was my favourite place to play. We used to make dens and houses from old bricks laid out in one or two layers in the form of a plan of different rooms, find old tins and bottles in which we would put tall, purple spiked, weed flowers and moon daisies that grew so prolifically on the waste ground, and make brooms from branches and leaves to sweep our 'house' clean.

I was christened in Trinity Church and went to Hannah Moore Infants until it was pulled down for the new police station. The Lord Mayor once came to a school service at Trinity church complete with horse and carriage. We then had to move to Hannah Moore School (Barleyfields) which is still by Gardiner's. Because it was the nearest school to the fairground caravan site in Gloucester Lane (off of West Street) we had one of the Henderson boys in our class for a short time.

I remember the lovely smell of toffee apples being made, coming from the shop in the next street on the corner of Clarence and Regent Street.

I had my ears pierced in Stocks the jewellers on the corner of Trinity Street and West Street and remember there used to be a chip shop in Trinity Street where you could get a bag of scrumps (small bits of batter). My friend, Jennifer Edwards lived in Trinity Street, and used to have a big throne-like room which was a toilet with a huge wooden seat.

I vaguely remember there being a murder in Trinity Street, and seeing a coloured lady hanging out of the bedroom window, throat cut and the blood staining the pavement.

There were no road markings on the crossroads between our street and Trinity Street, and we would frequently hear a heart stopping crash, as two cars would collide.

Peacocks in Clarence Road was one of my favourite places to shop, especially for the toys. It was later converted to a bingo hall and has now been demolished.

We had a Clarks pie shop on the main Clarence Road and I can still remember how the walking boards used to creak and flex when you entered. You always had to queue and a little Welsh lady with a huge smile used to serve you.

Around the corner in Waterloo Road the brewery used to stable their dray horses. The cobbles, which are still there today, were used to protect the road from the dray cart wheels and horses hooves. At the other end of Church Street, a rope works ran behind Catharine Street – where rope was strung out to dry along the yard.

Our doctor's surgery (Evans and Gunner) was on the corner of Barrow Road, where you would go and take a seat at the end of the queue and all move along one chair at a time till it was your turn (no receptionist or appointments then). When it was very busy you had to sit on the higher level and them move down the step to the lower level. It was always a friendly meeting place where people would catch up on the latest hatches, matches and dispatches.

Then came the council's sweeping decision to clear our 'slum' area to make way for a new road. My parents house was compulsorily purchased for a hundred pounds and we had to find a new home. We moved as near as we could, to Redfield, as did many others from Newtown. Some held out for more money and I remember a few odd houses left in Trinity Street, still occupied while all around them was being demolished. I used to walk home from Temple Colston School in Victoria Street, up through the remains of our area as it was slowly demolished. It seemed so sad, I wish now that I'd had a camera and taken some photographs. When it was hot I would stop and buy a Jubbly, an iced triangle, from the remaining shop in Barrow Road, break the top open and it would last me the rest of my journey home.

The new road never happened and instead they built three-storey houses by pouring concrete between two pieces of wood – I wonder if they will survive for over a hundred years – as our home had?'

Fancy dress in Regent Street to celebrate the Queen's Coronation in 1953. The image was taken looking towards Barrow Road, with Morley Terrace off to the right. At this time, eighty families lived in Regent Street.

The Freemasons Arms Hotel: The biggest and arguably Newtown's best pub sadly demolished in 1969. It was situated on the corner of Barrow Road and Regent Street and was known locally as the 'Spion Kop'. Fully licensed, it consisted of a smoke room, a public bar and a long bar. In the 1950s it was one of only a handful of Ushers pubs in the city. Reg and Beatrice Gwinnell were landlord and landlady from 1948 to 1957.

This building in Trinity Street was originally the garage of Greyhound Motors. They were the first company to start an express coach service in the country. It ran between Bristol and London and commenced in February 1925. Local bus services were also run and Greyhound became the main competitor of the mighty Bristol Tramways Company. In January 1936, Bristol Tramways acquired Greyhound and took over the garage. It was used as a bus and coach depot until the mid-1950s. The building is still standing and is now the only remaining landmark of old Newtown.

The Dove Inn was Newtown's last pub on the corner of Trinity Street and Church Street. Like the Freemasons it was fully licensed to sell wines and spirits as well as beer. Its location on the edge of the Newtown redevelopment zone appeared to make it a good candidate to survive the demolition. However, it was flattened in 1969/70 and today the site is a patch of waste ground near the Bristol to Bath cycle path.

The women and children of Trinity Street turned out in full for the Kings Silver Jubilee in 1935. The question is, where were all the men from the street?

The Engineers Tavern at No. 27 Barrow Road, on the corner of Hardinge Street. Just five doors along was another public house, the Millwrights Arms. The Engineers Tavern had been pulled down by 1965.

Hardinge Street, during Coronation time in 1953. Taken looking towards Wellesley Street, with Barrow Road behind the camera. The street's thirty-four houses would all be demolished by 1963, although the defunct carriage-way remained visible throughout the 1960s.

Loveday Builders, at No.76 Regent Street. By 14 December 1965, this former shop on the corner with Regent Terrace had become the office of K. Loveday, builders. In 1944 the shop was owned by Fred Thomas.

Millwrights Darts Team. The Millwrights Arms was situated at No. 37 Barrow Road and was a very popular haunt for local railway men. The darts team is seen here in the summer of 1937 on a day trip to the seaside. The landlord George Brooks is on the front row, far right. The location is thought to be Brighton.

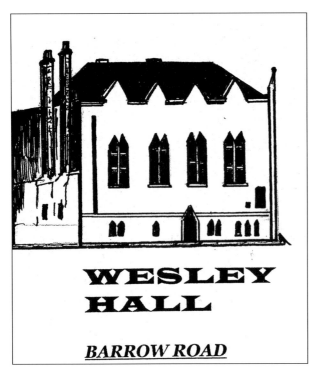

**WESLEY HALL**

**BARROW ROAD**

Wesley Hall, Newtown. Dating from 1888, its early inspiration came from Mr C. Parsons and members of the Old Market Street Wesleyan chapel. In its prime, it was noted for a thriving Sunday school and a successful Boys Brigade company. The Hall had been demolished by March 1969.

Wesley Hall and Barrow Road. The Wesley Hall stood on the corner of Barrow Road and Morley Terrace. Small boys peer round the corner as a member of the Girls Brigade poses with the Brigade colours. A small delivery van makes its way along Barrow Road from the Lawrence Hill direction. It is June, sometime in the 1950s. The sign above the door proclaims the times of services after the renovation and redecoration. Barrow Road was important enough to have white lines down the middle of the road and modern electric street lights.

An early 1950s image of a Wesley Hall crowd looking towards Barrow Road. Children from Wesley chapel line up in Morley Terrace. In the background is Bill Sparke's shop.

A coach trip from Wesley Hall. Nearly all local churches and chapels organized church or Sunday School outings once a year in the summer, usually to Weston Super Mare. Five vehicles belonging to Eagle Coaches of Goulter Street, Barton Hill, line up in Morley Terrace, to take Wesley chapel parishioners on their annual trip to the seaside in the early 1950s.

Wesley Hall Boys Brigade, leading a parade in the early 1950s. The location is thought to be Regent Street. Bands and marching through the streets were an important part of Boys Brigade life.

The Wesley Hall Girls Brigade marching in the early 1950s.

The Foresters Arms was situated at No.16 Clarence Street, on the corner with Church Street. When this photograph was taken on 14 December 1965, the pub was in the ownership of Courage Breweries. The landlord in 1944 was Alf Hooper.

The interior of the Foresters Arms. The pub had an unusual round bar. Taken on the 8 September 1967, the picture is typical of the very spartan design of local pubs in the 1960s. The pub was purchased by the Bristol Corporation and demolished in March 1969.

Newtown in 1965. A revealing picture taken from the new flats, as Newtown teetered on the brink of almost total demolition. On the left is Morley Terrace with the Wesley Hall rising above Barrow Road. On the right is Melbourne Terrace. Today the spine-road link to Lawrence Hill roundabout dominates the foreground.

Newtown Tavern was situated at No. 60 Regent Street on the corner with Morley Terrace. Although by now a Courage pub, it still displayed a sign proudly advertising George's Beers. The date is 14 December 1965. The landlord in 1955 was Fred Peglar.

Bill Sparke's shop in Barrow Road, taken on 8 September 1967. This was the last shop standing at the Newtown end of the road, at No. 45. Adorning the shop are advertisements for Senior Service, Guards, Players, Bristol and Capstan cigarettes – and not a government health warning in sight!

Barrow Road shed was opened by the Midland Railway Company in 1873 to replace an earlier shed. The thirteen-arch bridge carrying Barrow Road spanned the railway yard. This photograph was taken in the late 1930s. LMS Black 5 No 5261 (later BR No 45261) steams out from the shed to work its next duty. A line of smaller ex-Midland Railway engines can be seen behind. The shed closed on 20 November 1965, the building was demolished in 1967 and the Midland Line closed on 3 January 1970.

Harris' secondhand shop at No. 5 Barrow Road. It was run by G. Harris when this photograph was taken on 17 September 1965. The shop was demolished in April 1969.

Barrow Road, September 1964. The junction with Lawrence Hill is behind the camera. Centre is Walter Love's hairdresser and tobacconist on the corner of a footpath which ran behind Catharine Street. This Newtown end of Barrow Road was all to be pulled down by 1970. Note the Ford Anglia, left, which for many workers was their first car. The advertisements on the wall included a picture of Harold Wilson who was about to lead the Labour Party to victory in the October 1964 General Election.

Regent Terrace. A picture which symbolised the plight of Newtown in 1967. Today this row would probably be valued and protected. Those living in the properties on the south of the terrace, had a good view of the extensive railway activity in between Barrow Road and St Philips station. Today this site is the part of the cycle path.

Demolition of Regent Terrace. Most of Newtown was demolished between 1967 and 1969. Here we see Bristol Corporation workmen hard at work demolishing No. 17 Regent Terrace on the corner with Melbourne Terrace. The usual method was the ball and chain. One or two hits and the old Victorian terrace houses collapsed in a pile of dust. This house had previously been the home of Miss Patience Haley.

A street party in Newtown. Tables had been brought out into the street and covered with clean white sheets. The limited amount of food on the table suggests that this may have been VE Day 1945. The location is thought to be Trinity Street.

# *Five*
# Lawrence Hill

Lawrence Hill takes its name from a leper hospital which was dedicated to St Lawrence. This stood roughly where today a roundabout is situated.

Built in 1208 on land given by the future King John, it was adjacent to the main London Road. The buildings consisted of a chapel, hospital block and 'great house'.

After Henry VIIIs dissolution of the Church, the buildings were sold to Sir Ralph Sadler. He rebuilt the site as a fine mansion and it was here that Queen Elizabeth I stopped on her famous visit to Bristol in 1574. By 1700 it seems that all remains of the house and outbuildings had vanished, although people could still remember seeing part of the outer wall near the Easton Road vicarage.

In the 1950s, Lawrence Hill boasted traders of all types, a large range of pubs and a key asset for the patch; its own railway station. The buildings were a real mix of styles and scales, reflecting the haphazard expansion of Bristol eastwards. Walking to town from Redfield you would pass one fascinating unbroken line of shops and pubs. This eclectic mix survived the Blitz on Bristol but in the 1960s this scene was to change in the most dramatic of ways.

In the same year that the Beatles released their first record, Bristol's planners revealed their futuristic twenty-year vision for Lawrence Hill, Easton and Newtown. This 1962 plan outlined the concept of a new 'Super Suburb'. It was out with the Victorian past and in with modern, bold 1960s ideas.

The plan revolved around skyscraper flats, a revolutionary shopping precinct and an urban motorway called the Outer Circuit Road. A vast chunk of the area which stood in 1962 would be swept away. Councillors saw the plan as a bold attack on the area's problems. These were outlined as poor housing above all but also an outmoded road pattern, haphazard industrial development and a lack of open space. However the plan seemed alien to a community where residents could stroll up and down their road and chat with neighbours over the fence.

The plan dismissed the Victorian and Georgian structures as 'crumbling buildings' clearly not worthy to survive next to the gleaming 1960s architecture. A balance between restoring and retaining the best of the old and incorporating it with the new was not on the agenda. The general feeling at the time was of a desire for change, and a political will to create a 'new, modern Britain' (and a new, modern Bristol). Car ownership was rapidly increasing, while ownership of domestic appliances such as televisions was accelerating. At this time there was some popular support for the view that the old Victorian landscape belonged to an age of poverty, unemployment and generally poor living conditions. Spurred on by this and with little opposition, the plans became increasingly aggressive and strident. One example of this was the

Outer Circuit Road, Bristol's big transport idea in the 1960s. It was described in 1964 as the city's 'inter-district freeway'. It was to be carved through many of Bristol's inner suburbs and at Lawrence Hill its impact was to be especially dramatic. Lawrence Hill was to be broken up by an intersection: a vast roundabout complex complete with elevated sections and subways. In addition, there was to be a really novel feature. A shopping centre was to be built inside the traffic island. Reports at the time described this as being styled like a three-tiered wedding cake!

The contrast with the Lawrence Hill of 1962 could not have been greater. One local resident at the time described the artist's impression as 'like if a giant spaceship had landed on Lawrence Hill'.

Quite simply, the planners were aiming for nothing less than the complete transformation of an area they viewed as a Victorian eyesore. This was the view forcibly presented to locals as a *fait accompli*. So followed the years of transition. Gradually and steadily, familiar shops were boarded up and left to decay pending the demolition crews. Adjacent houses were cleared in droves and historic pubs fell silent. By 1972 a great deal had gone including the authorities' appetite for the Outer Circuit Road. Under pressure from various fronts, the authorities abandoned the grand plan but not before the Lawrence Hill Roundabout had been completed. It was still vast in size but with no shopping centre in the middle as planned. There were barren grass mounds and a feeling that a huge, soul-less void had been created between the Packhorse and West Street. Many people still view it as an appalling piece of 1960s planning.

However in the 1960s, tower blocks, massive roads and new 'neighbourhood units' were the order of the day. All over Bristol from Kingsdown to Totterdown, the bulldozers moved to create the authority's 'brave new world'. Today the mistakes and excesses of the 1960s are fully recognized. Lawrence Hill with it's roundabout remains a classic example of that 1960s thinking.

The junction of Easton Road and Lawrence Hill, viewed from Clarence Road. The umbrella shop can be seen on the left, followed by the Blackmoors Head. The triangular buildings in the centre date from 1900. Before that stood Garton's Brewery which dated from 1824. The brewery ingredients went in on the Easton Road side and the finished products went out on the other in Lawrence Hill. Only the left hand side of that building now remains, (now the LA Gym). St Lawrence Church can also be seen.

Brains Cycles at No. 13 Lawrence Hill, the Clarence Road end. A well-respected Bristol cycle shop, which started around 1916. An establishment used by generations of cyclists, it continued to trade throughout the redevelopment. Andy Jones, one of the co-authors, last visited the shop in June 1979. It is fair to say it was past its best by this time and it closed shortly afterwards.

The Morning Star Garage. Mr Jones commenced charabanc operations in 1919, operating under the name Morning Star, and, by the early 1920s had established several express and local excursion services as well as private hire and taxi operation. The vehicles were garaged at No. 55 Lawrence Hill. The garage is seen here in the late 1920s, along with the vehicles of G.H. Hill, a fruit and potato merchant who also used the garage. In 1948 Morning Star amalgamated with several other Bristol coach firms to become Wessex Coaches Ltd.

The Waverley Vaults at No. 83 Lawrence Hill. It became a pub in the 1890s and was a few doors along from Wellington Street. The building was situated between Sheppard and Hall's ironmongers and a Co-operative furnishing warehouse. All were demolished for the roundabout.

The Three Tuns at No. 65 Lawrence Hill. This was a popular pub and one of the last buildings to be pulled down for the roundabout. It was near the junction of Lawrence Hill with Wellington Street. In the late-eighteenth century it was run by a William Hawkins. If it survived today it would be inside the roundabout!

Rawlings, at No. 121 Lawrence Hill. With St Lawrence Church on one side, and a little alley known as Unity Place on the other, the Rawlings family ran their newspaper business here from 1910 until around 1946. Later it was Poole's the chemist.

In the 1920s, part of the church's pinnacle crashed through two floors of their shop, narrowly missing Albert Rawlings. The family complained to the vicar, whose only comment was 'it must be an act of God!' He promised to have it removed, but forty years later it was still in the yard. It is now in the family garden. The roundabout is now on the site.

The staff of 'The Electric Spark' pose on Lawrence Hill Bridge in 1965.

St Lawrence Church. An elegant, beautiful structure dating from 1885. Its admirable architectural style (imitation fourteenth-century Gothic) made it a notable landmark in the area. The building's real gem was a very pretty tower and a short spire. The fine lines of the Glass House pub are also prominent in this classic Lawrence Hill image. St Lawrence Church was largely demolished in 1956, although the lower section of the exterior wall fronting Lawrence Hill remained in place throughout the 1960s; a poignant reminder of the church and a once-fine building.

The splendid and elaborate interior of St Lawrence Church.. The church could seat 718 people. Before the opening in 1885, the congregation had met opposite in the Charlton Hall. The building was renovated in 1906 and was damaged in the 1940/41 Blitz. However, the church hall behind the main building was destroyed in the air raids and the caretaker was killed. The last couple to be married in St Lawrence were Mr and Mrs Coles, on 26 April 1954. The church was closed shortly afterwards when the Anglican authorities controversially declared it 'surplus to requirements'.

The Glass House Hotel. A stylish, ornate and well-proportioned structure. This impressive pub ended its days as a Courage establishment; before that it had been a Simonds outlet. In the 1930s, Roger's ales were sold, while around 1900, Anglo-Bavarian brews were on offer. The Glass House was home to various clubs and was a popular venue for wedding receptions. Its destruction in February 1969 was a sad loss for Lawrence Hill.

The Co-operative store in Lawrence Hill (1887-1967). The Co-op came to Lawrence Hill in 1887 when their first choice of shop was agreed verbally with the landlord. However, local traders put in a higher bid which was accepted – just one of the 'dirty tricks' used to try and keep out the Co-op. However, they were so successful that they were able instead to build their own store on the corner of Leadhouse Lane. In 1890 it became the HQ for the Bristol Co-operative Society. This also provided coal, a bakery, a drapery, a Boots store and a funeral service. In the 1960s, the council wanted to demolish it for the redevelopment. A price was agreed with a promise of a new store to be built inside the new roundabout. The shop was pulled down but the new shop was cancelled, leaving the Co-op high and dry. The old shop site is still left empty today.

The chip shop at No. 1 Berkeley Street. On the corner of Berkeley Street and Leadhouse Road stood Edwin Tomkie's fish and chip shop. The shop featured some lovely green glazed tiling to the bottom of the building. At the other end of Berkeley Street stood the entrance gates to the Bristol Omnibus Company Central Repair Works. This photograph was taken on 17 March 1966. The building was later demolished and became part of the site of Berkeley House, the new offices for Bristol Omnibus Company which replaced the offices at St Augustine's Parade.

Berkeley Street. This view looks towards the bus depot (originally Bristol Wagon and Carriage Works), with Lawrence Hill behind the camera. Berkeley Street was pulled down during 1967 for the building of Berkeley House. No evidence of the street remains today.

The Rose at No. 29 Berkeley Street. Built before 1880, it was originally a grocery shop before becoming a newsagents. In around 1920 it turned into the Rose off-licence. Like the rest of the street it was demolished in 1967. Note the distinctive low stone wall which curled around into Lawrence Hill.

Knights, No. 141 Lawrence Hill. This tobacconist shop was run by Mrs Minnie Knight from 1911 until the early 1950s It was next door to the Earl Russell public house.

The Prince Albert off-licence, at No. 1A Croydon Street, with Leadhouse Road off to the left. An architecturally interesting, almost triangular building, originally next to four dwellings known as Roach's Cottages. Mrs Florence Ethel Watkins ran the off-licence for its last twenty-five years of existence. By 1965, the Prince Albert and most of Croydon Street had vanished to make way for the redevelopment.

Lawrence Hill/Newtown, *c*. 1968. The photograph was taken from Kingsmarsh House. Lawrence Hill is centre right, with Holy Trinity church to the left of the picture. Barrow Road is centre left. As is evident, much had been demolished by this time. Note the three houses surviving in Catharine Street, near the junction of Barrow Road and Lawrence Hill. The bottom of the picture shows Henry and Hardinge Streets, cleared of their houses. The Lawrence Hill Health Centre and the roundabout would be built in the foreground.

The Earl Russell public house in 1985 At this time, it was owned by Whitbread Brewery. Next door the old coal office has become an office for Warners (Bristol) Ltd, building contractors. This office was demolished in 1998 to make a wider access into the new supermarket, constructed on the old Lawrence Hill railway yard.

The Bristol and South Wales Union Railway opened a station at Lawrence Hill on the 8 September 1863. 107 years later on the 26 May 1970, this photograph was taken showing the buildings on Platform 1 which were part of the original 1863 station, and the unique booking office on the bridge. The station was extended from two platforms to four in 1891, and new buildings were constructed on Platforms 2, 3 and 4. A wooden footbridge linked the platforms together. The station master in 1944 was T.C. Olding.

When the station was rebuilt in 1891, a fine new signal box was built to replace the earlier one situated further up the line. At the same time the line was quadrupled to take the South Wales to London trains which were now running through Bristol, following the opening of the Severn Tunnel on 1 September 1886. The station still boasted gas lights when this photograph was taken on 26 May 1970. The box was closed in 1970, when the Bristol Panel was opened at Temple Meads.

Lawrence Hill had excellent goods facilities and this fine red brick goods shed was built by the Great Western Railway Company to handle local deliveries. By the mid-1960s, the shed was being used solely by the Aberthaw Cement Company for the unloading of bagged cement. A silo was built adjoining the shed to handle liquid cement. The goods shed was demolished in November 1997.

The goods yard at Lawrence Hill was always very busy. Its principle traffic was coal. In 1944 the following coal merchants were all using the yard: H.E. Coole and Company, E.E. Mills, Huntley and Co Ltd and the Bristol Co-operative Society Ltd. By the 1970s the coal had finished and the principle traffics were cement, scrap metal and bricks. The yard closed in the early 1990s.

Electric Spark, 1926-1970s. Newicks opened their first shop in Clouds Hill Road in 1896. This, the second shop, known as Newicks, came in 1926. It was not until 1937 that both shops were called The Electric Spark, named after the trams that turned outside the other St George shop. Their daughter married Leonard Nicholls and they took over the shops. The Newick family also owned a candle-making factory in Old Market.

Gingells shop at No. 204 Lawrence Hill. The Gingells ran this butcher's shop from 1915-1982 and it was a butchers previously to that. During the war, rabbits were a popular dish. They collected them from Wiltshire and over 1,000 were sold each week. George Gingell could skin four of them in a minute. The family retired in 1982 and bought a farm at Awkley near Tockington. Stuckeys was next door (house furnishing) and later supplying menswear. It closed in the late 1970s.

Woodburys Pet Stores was situated at No. 202 Lawrence Hill. Even in the early 1980s the shop boasted a fine array of enamel signs advertising Spratts dog biscuits. The shop sold pet foods and accessories, baby budgerigars and was the only shop in the area selling goldfish. The shop also sold fishing nets for catching tiddlers at St Georges Park Lake.

The Packhorse Inn. Eleanor Silverthorn left land in 1757 known as Ten Acres which included everything between the London Road (now Lawrence Hill) and what we know as Silverthornes Lane, to her daughter Elizabeth who was married to Thomas Crisp. Crisp rebuilt structures already there, and turned it into a tavern with a brewery behind It was not known as the Packhorse until 1793. It takes its name from Packhorse Lane (Ducie Road). William Herapath the famous analytical chemist who was involved in many famous murder trials was born here.

Ron Lovells, on 3 July 1964, by the Midland Railway bridge at 146 Lawrence Hill – what a fantastic shop! Ron Lovell's shop sold wool, newspapers, tobacco and sweets. There were cigarette advertisements, big glass bottles full of sweets and posters on the left window and door for Billy Smart's Circus, which was appearing on Durdham Down at the time.

David Griffiths and Sons shop at 144 Lawrence Hill, standing empty on 3 July 1964. The shop had primarily been a fishmongers selling wet fish, but it also sold greengrocery and fresh fruit. Shop windows were usually whitened when shops were unoccupied.

Numbers 136-146 Lawrence Hill, 3 July 1964. The wall of the railway bridge still exists today but all these shops were pulled down to create 'green space' around Baynton House flats. The junction of Lawrence Hill and Leadhouse Road is behind the camera.

Kingsburys in 1964, on the corner of Lawrence Hill and Charlton Street. The Baynton House block of flats was later built off right. Note that Kingsbury's had moved with the times – there is an advertisement for Birds Eye frozen foods. This 1872 building and indeed rank (Augustus Buildings) would be replaced by trees, grass and garaging for the new flats.

Charlton Street Chapel. Charlton Street ran from Lawrence Hill to Rich's Lane. In the middle of the street stood the Charlton Gospel Hall. This view was taken on 3 July 1964 just prior to demolition to make way for the building of Baynton House. A fine array of 1950s and '60s cars can be seen, as well as an electric street light which had been converted from gas. In the background to the extreme right, part of Barrow Road Bridge and one of the gasholders at Days Road can be seen. A small section of the cobbled Rich's Lane still exists today.

The Wellesely Arms in Lawrence Hill. A mens outing during 1915, including Mr Henry Provis who was on leave from the army during the First World War. He is sixth from the left on the front row along with his dad, who lived at No. 10 Charlton Street.

The Bargain Stores was a drapers and house furnishers at Nos. 80 and 82 Lawrence Hill. The name of its previous owner still appeared above the shop door: John Swaish, Justice of the Peace and former Lord Mayor, who had many pawnbroker shops in Bristol. His first shop on Lawrence Hill was at No. 116 back in 1879, moving here in 1890. The shop became the Bargain Stores in 1943 operating as a tailor, house furnishers and jewellers shop. Mr Porter was manager and partner. It was demolished for the roundabout. Wellesley Street off left.

The 'Little Black Horse' inn. Typical of many small beer houses in the east Bristol area, the 'L.B.H.' was tucked away in the middle of Wellesley Street. This mid-Victorian Street was named after the famous soldier and Prime Minister, Arthur Wellesley, the first Duke of Wellington. The Street was demolished in 1961/62 for the building of the Kingsmarsh House block of flats.

Wookey the chemist, at No. 24 Lawrence Hill. The name 'Brunswick House' and the date '1857' were chiseled into the stone up near the roof. Sydney Wookey came to this shop on the corner of Barrow Road in 1955 and stayed until the end in the 1970s. He paid £3,750 for the shop and received just £4,250 from the council.

Inside Wookey's. Very modern for its time, it probably had as much space for women's cosmetics as it did for medicines, plus two chairs for people to sit on while they waited for prescriptions.

Lawrence Hill was a great place for shopping. Look at this line of shops, taken on 17 September 1965. At No. 20 is Bollom Ltd, dyers and cleaners, at No. 18 is Foster Brothers Ltd, outfitters, at No 16 is G.H. Webb and Co Ltd, provision merchants and at No. 14 is Pearks Dairies Ltd, grocers. All these shops were demolished to make way for the Lawrence Hill roundabout and new housing.

Numbers 2-14 Lawrence Hill in 1965. Continuing the shopping line to Clarence Road, the Bunch of Grapes public house is the last building on the right. All demolished by April 1969.

The interior of the Bunch of Grapes. A fine view of the public bar, taken on 8 September 1967. The number one record on this day was *The Last Waltz* by Engelbert Humperdinck.

The exterior of the Bunch of Grapes at Nos. 54-56 Clarence Road, pictured on 8 September 1967. To the right of the pub is the doorway which led to the Wessex Coach Station. This site had been Shepherds, destroyed during the Bristol Blitz. The public house managed to survive. In 1944 the landlady was Mrs Florence Mary O' Gorman. Note the bus stop.

Central Lawrence Hill. A revealing 1964 panorama of the area which was pulled down for the new flats and roundabout. The stretch on the right is between Barrow Road and Wellesley Street and was all gone by 1969. In the far distance is the Co-op and the Church Road end of Lawrence Hill. The building on the extreme right (which was on the corner of Barrow Road) housed the doctors practice of Doctors Evans and Gunner. This red-bricked building survived the 1960s demolition and remained in isolation until pulled down to make way for the 1977 Lawrence Hill Health Centre.

Central Lawrence Hill in late 1971. A Morris Oxford travels east towards Church Road. Today this site would be in the middle of the roundabout. The neat Easton Road Board School is prominent, but its days are numbered. The school is overshadowed by the new tower blocks Emra House (right) and Twinnell House (left). This is a picture which captures what Lawrence Hill was like during the latter years of the redevelopment.

Hemmings Parade. Lawrence Hill is off to the left, with the Midland railway line in the foreground. The front row of houses is Hemmings Parade. This terrace was demolished between 1965 and 1969, although the adjacent houses (Brentry Avenue) were retained. In the 1970s a rank of distinctive modern houses were built on the site of the Parade. Note that Gaunts Ham Park and the Barton Hill flats are in the background.

Number 121 Lawrence Hill in 1970. At this time this building was quite isolated – a relic from the old Lawrence Hill. On the point of being pulled down, it had formerly been Rawlings and latterly Poole's chemist. Note the 'step up' pavement, the remains of St Lawrence church and the new flats in the background.

Latty's chemist, 134 Lawrence Hill. The old chemist on the corner of Charlton Street was run by Mr Poole in its final years. But locals always called it Latty's chemist, after the gentleman, William Latty, who ran it from 1925-1957. On the left of the image is the grocers and café which was run by Harold and Kay Kingsbury. They later ran a café next to the Earl Russell public house.

Baynton House in Lawrence Hill – the new tower block taking shape in 1964. Kingsbury's shop, on the corner of Charlton Street, was soon to be demolished. The planners were determined that no old buildings would stand next to the flats. Many locals would come to feel that a corner shop was of more use than a communal patch of grass. Both Baynton House and the adjacent larger Kingsmarsh House were completed in 1965. The first flats were let in June 1965.

Lawrence Hill looking towards Clarence Road, in the late 1960s. Near the camera on the left had been Kerswell's, Bristol's oldest cycle makers. Established in 1887, Kerswell's shop at No. 56 Lawrence Hill was demolished in 1966. The two and three storey buildings on the immediate right were knocked down in 1971 for the outer lane of the roundabout. Half of the four storey rank was demolished in 1984.

The Glass House Hotel, as seen on 17 September 1965. The Co-op is on the right, with the ruins of St Lawrence Church to the left. The demolition of the Glass House for the roundabout brought home to many locals the scope and scale of the Lawrence Hill redevelopment.

A model of New Easton. The planners dramatic, new vision was given the green light in the 1966 development plan. The big white highway on the right of the map is the Parkway M32 motorway link to Broadmead (off right). The Lower Ashley Road roundabout is at the bottom of this model, while the Lawrence Hill roundabout is at the top. Linking these two vast intersections is the Easton part of the Outer Circuit Road, This link was the only section of the Outer Circuit Road to be built and is now called Easton Way. This model clearly shows that the Outer Circuit Road was to pass over the shopping centre inside the Lawrence Hill roundabout on its way to Totterdown.

The Croydon Street and Leadhouse Road area, 1965. The 'man from the Ministry' views an area in transition. Note the brand new Lawrence Hill tower blocks (Kingsmarsh and Baynton Houses) in the background. The area on the right would become the site of new housing and the roundabout. A new Croydon Street was later built but on a different alignment than the original; Leadhouse Road vanished totally.

The roundabout: 'The brave New World'. In 1964 Councillors were enthusing about plans for a giant three-tiered roundabout that was in fact a shopping centre! It finally opened (without the shops) in 1973 and this picture from that time gives some impression of its scale. Over 150 buildings (houses, shops and pubs) were demolished to make way for this roundabout. Proposed in 1962 and opened in 1973, traffic lights were added in 1994. (See introduction to Lawrence Hill).

Church Road, 1971. On the extreme right is Hodders butchers at No. 2 Church Road. Next door is a sweet shop, later a grocers. Then Morton Street with Chandlers chemist on the corner (dating from around 1886). Followed by Prings, Thomas Street, the Kings Arms and Rawlings. Palfreys and the buildings on the corner of Cobden Street brought you to the Russell Town Congregational Church.

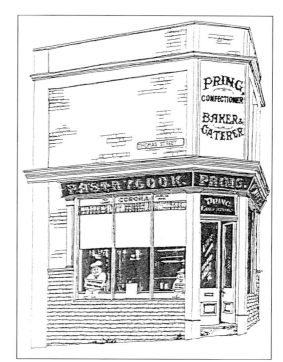

Prings the baker at No. 8 Church Road. Edwin Ford Pring opened this shop around 1893 on the corner of Thomas Street. When Mr Pring died, Ernie Sharp took over. The shop was later owned by Herbert's. The shop was noted for its glass fascias and gilded lettering. This elaborate design was balanced by a very simple wooden shop front. In Pring's day it was considered one of Bristol's best pastry shops.

Whites, 12-14 Church Road, next door to the Kings Arms. This shop hasn't changed much over the years. Today it is Rawlings the Furnishers (and has been since the late-1950s). It was the Co-op from 1943-1956. Before that it was the Blue Saving Stamp Co, Miss Mabel Whites, Scammells and the Russell Town Drapers, which, from 1886 had always been a drapery store.

The Cobden Arms, at No. 4 Cobden Street, near the junction with Church Road. This off-licence was situated a few doors down from the Russell Town School Rooms. Closed by 1966, this rather elegant building had been demolished by the end of 1968.

Russell Town School Rooms. This building in Cobden Street was used by the Russell Town Congregational Church for Sunday School classes, and activities such as billiards, table tennis and concerts. Originally opened in 1869 by the British and Foreign School Society, it was later rented to the Bristol School Board. After 1905 it was a girl's and infant's school. This gloomy, grey building was demolished in the mid 1960s and replaced by the Cashmore House flats.

Russell Town Congregational Church, Cobden Street. This structure fronted Church Road and was built on land provided by Christopher Godwin. Originally, the church met in a house in nearby Jane Street. The new building cost £3,500 and was dedicated on 2 April 1868. The Revd James Trebilco was an early high-profile vicar, while in the 1950s it was part of the Redfield United Front of churches. Closed in 1968 (for a new church in Ducie Road), the building was finally demolished in 1976.

Russell Town Congregational Church, pictured here for the wedding of Doreen Sheeley and Ron Parsons on 17 June 1967. The boarded-up Cobden Arms is in the background. The number one record on this day was *A Whiter Shade of Pale* by Procol Harum.

Max Williams had three shops, at Nos. 5, 7 and 9 Church Road, near to Lawrence Hill station. No. 5 was the toy and model shop – the finest in Bristol and perhaps one of the finest in the country. No. 7 was a bicycle shop and No. 9 a moped shop. Bicycles and mopeds were sold and repaired. This photograph was taken in August 1987 after the bicycle and moped shops had been closed. The bicycle shop then reopened across the road under the ownership of Max's son.

Inside Max Williams shop. By the mid-1960s, Max Williams had become a mecca for model railway enthusiasts. It sold absolutely everything they required. However, as well as selling Tri-ang and Hornby Railways, the shop also sold Dinky and Corgi Toys, Matchbox, Spot-On, Budgie, Mecanno, Scalectrix, Lego and Airfix. Here we see the inside of the shop, in 1993, during the last week before it closed, as usual packed to the rafters with stock.

The interior of the Globe Cinema, as seen in the 1950s. Looking from the screen, the cheaper seats downstairs looked okay, but the balcony seats were far more desirable, and you could see the openings where the films were projected.

The Globe Cinema, Church Road, 1914-1974. The Pugsley family built the Globe in 1914, and later went on to build or buy many other cinemas in Bristol. Although Joseph Pugsley was the owner, it was actually run by his eldest son George and, much later, Oliver his youngest. Joseph never saw his movies and died just before the 'talkies' arrived. He had gradually gone blind. The theatre could seat 1,172 but some of this seating was lost along with its original frontage when major alterations were made in the 1930s. The cinema closed after it's final viewing, Walt Disney's *The Aristocats*, on 6 January 1974. Jane Street off left.

Ruby Helder, 1890-1938, the international opera star known as 'The Lady Tenor'. Born Emma Jane Holden at No. 7 Brooklyn Terrace, her family moved to 114. Within a few years of her birth, her father became the landlord of the Glass House on Lawrence Hill. Here she would practice her singing, and later she went on to train at the Guildhall School of Music. At a very early age she became famous all over the world. Even Enrico Caruso was impressed by her unusual voice. She died in 1938, aged just forty-eight. A plaque was erected in her memory at Walker Close, just off Easton Road on June 15 2001.

St Lawrence AFC. The season was 1913-1914 and we think that one of the players is a member of the Smale family. Can you name any of the players or the vicars?

Palfrey the butchers, at No. 16 Church Road. Over 100 years later the shop is still in business, although now it is a café and takeaway. Worthy Palfrey bought the business from Mr Abel Willis, having worked day and night to raise the money needed. Using a horse for deliveries and later horse and cart, the business grew. They sold lamb and beef, the beasts were kept in pens in the backyard until needed, and then killed on the premises. Albert took over from his dad and ran the business with his wife Mabel, who he met when she worked next door in White's. Son Michael would be the third generation and now his son in law runs it.

# Victorian Cellars

These cellars were created when the railway company needed to heighten the road because of line improvements along with the new Barrow Road engine shed and siding complex. The shops which at that time stood between the Packhorse and Ducie Road disappeared underground as did the old Packhorse Inn. Still intact as they were, five or six arched cellars were also built. Only the first went all across the road. The others were bricked up half way, to allow the other side to be used for small businesses.

Underground, the old shops still had their glass fronts and at least one Victorian lamp, that would disappear in the 1950s when the shop-fronts were bricked up for security, with the exception of one sash window, used in the last war as an unofficial air raid shelter.

In the only arched cellar to go all the way across the road, two old wooden horse troughs still remain, and above that is another small chamber leading out to the public toilets. This was the only light a horse saw until they went out to work.

'Going underground': Andy Jones and Dave Stephenson find just one unbricked window.

Note the old horse troughs and remains of cloth to stop the wind, and protect the horses.

# Six
# Moorfields

Unlike Lawrence Hill or Newtown, Moorfields is not a name commonly used today. The area known as Moorfields was always a relatively small patch, as some said a 'bit of a backwater' in between Lawrence Hill and Redfield/Whitehall.

Historically there are two angles. Firstly the huddle of basic early nineteenth-century dwellings erected by Solomon Moore, centered around Moorfields Square and adjacent to Church Road. These were demolished in 1930. Secondly, the 1870s Moorfields estate, the hundreds of houses in uniform terraces which revolved around Dean lane (Russell Town Avenue). With its imposing school, its corner shops, off-licences and mission halls, this very working-class area survived as a distinct community until redevelopment came in the 1950s and '60s.

Wally Ball recalls, 'I was brought up in Moorfields during the First World War and I remember those days and the 1920s well. My childhood memories are of rows of terraced houses, smoke from their chimneys and streets full of children playing. I can also see those small general stores which were on every street corner.

The days after the First World War were very hard. These were the days of the depression, with unemployment and poverty rife. Of course there was no Welfare State in those days, the pawnbroker being vital to the survival of many. It was said that everyone was in the same boat – broke!

I recall vividly the selection of street traders and entertainers that ventured up Dean Lane. The rag and bone man, the Welsh cockle woman and the barrel organ man, to name just three.

From Bishop Street it was only a short walk to the Barton Hill Baths and the Globe Cinema – a wonderful place.'

After the Second World War, Moorfields was declared a zone for redevelopment and the first Compulsory Purchase Order was issued in 1956.

David Cheesley recalls: 'Around 1963, I used to play with friends in the Russell Town Avenue area. At this time, the remaining boarded-up houses in Canon Street, Bishop Street, Procter Street, Deacon Street, Dean Street and Chapter Street were being demolished. When the houses had finally been cleared, the deserted old roads made a perfect race track for us on our bikes. The only buildings left standing on this side of Russell Town Avenue were Alfred J. Rees sheet metal works in Bishop Street and the Ventures Youth Club in Chapter Street. This had been St Saviour's Mission Hall. On the other side, Mr Lockier's house remained next to a derelict site that had been Cattybrook Street. Between here and Lawrence Hill Station was Pugsleys scrap yard.

A tower block was built on the site of Moorfields Place in Church Road, but surprisingly no new housing came to Russell Town Avenue. The bulk of the area, the site of all those houses and small shops, was given over to the new St George Comprehensive School which opened in 1970. The 1900 school buildings were however retained and remain a link to the old Moorfields which vanished.

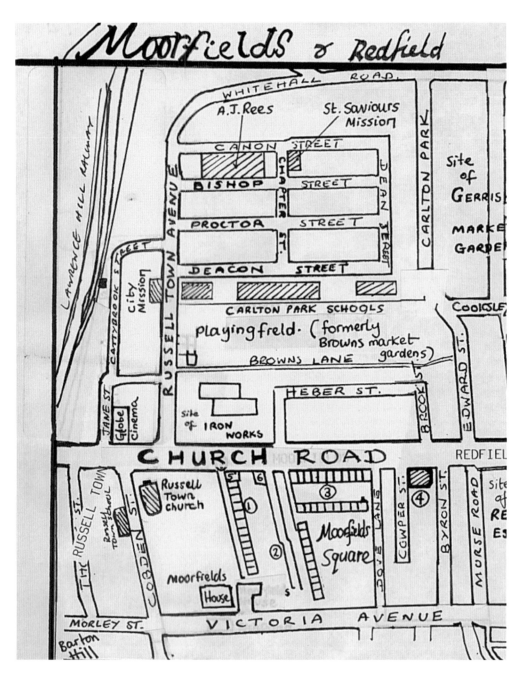

KEY: (Not to Scale)
1. Providence Place    3. Moorfields Place
2. Clarence Place      4. St. Matthews

A map of Moorfields and Redfield, 1929.

Moorfields House. An imposing and notable eighteenth-century house, with a commanding view to Church Road. In red brick with limestone dressings, it was built in the mid-Georgian style. In the 1840s it was known as Nelson House and from the 1880s to the 1950s it was the vicarage of Christ Church, Barton Hill. Note the middle semi-circular arched first-floor window.

Moorfields House (rear elevation). In the nineteenth-century, the house was noted for its spacious grounds. To the rear of the house was a very large fishpond, which had previously been an early reservoir. This was covered in when Victoria Square (later Avenue) was built. Since the late 1950s the house has been used by Shiners Builders Merchants as a store.

Church Road. An Edwardian shot, taken from the location of Shiner's Garage today. On the left is the turning into Dean Lane (renamed Russell Town Avenue in the 1920s). The shop on the corner of the junction was Montague Hedges pawnbrokers. This shop was pulled down in the 1950s for road widening. The distinctive rank on the left was dominated for many years by Hamiltons. This departmental store provided tailoring, house furnishing and prams, plus radio and electrical items.

The Moorfields section of Church Road in the 1920s. Looking from the corner of Dean Lane (Russell Town Avenue). The building on the extreme right is the Shepherds Rest public house. The next major building on the left is another public house, the Forge Hammer. This was separated from the main rank (Moorfields Place) by an alleyway which led to Moorfields Square. Moorfields Place and the two public houses were demolished between 1956 and '64 for the building of Moorfields House tower block which was opened in 1966.

The Pugsley family. Joseph Pugsley was the founder of the scrap metal business. Born in 1856 in North Devon, his first premises were at Cheese Lane in 1892, later moving to Midland Road. By 1903 he had purchased land at Cattybrook Street in Moorfields. This is also where he would build the Globe Cinema. They moved to selling second-hand machinery including steam wagons. The business was taken over by his sons George, William, Edward and Frederick and later by children from his second marriage, Oliver and daughter Winifred. Later they had a yard at Stoke Gifford. Interesting telegraphic address – 'Piston. Bristol.'

Pugsley's Ironworks. This building in Russell Town Avenue previously belonged to the Pugsley family and was known as Pugsley's Cattybrook Ironworks. The origin of the works dates back to the early nineteenth-century when an iron forge and rolling mill were built on land adjoining three cottages. By the 1870s it was known as the Wainbrook Ironworks. Pugsley's vacated the site in the early 1970s. The buildings are now part of Lawrence Hill Industrial Estate.

J. Pugsley & Sons Ltd. Two of the company's vehicles seen here parked in Russell Town Avenue. They were either arriving or leaving with second-hand machinery, sometime in the 1960s.

The Beaufort Works in Bishop Street. The unmistakable works of Alfred J. Rees. Off left is Russell Town Avenue with Chapter Street right. Originally a glue, gum and size works, in the 1900s it became Rees' Coach Works. By the 1960s, Alfred J Rees were car body repairers for the British Motor Corporation. Demolished in 1972 the site lay derelict for ten years until sports courts were laid out for St George School. The remaining roadway of Bishop Street disappeared at this time.

The Dean Lane City Mission. This was halfway along the present day Russell Town Avenue. Bristol City Mission Society was founded in 1826 to communicate religious knowledge to the poorer areas of the city. By 1900, this red brick structure had been built in Moorfields. Soon afterwards Arthur Shrubsall became the preacher/pastor, a well known figure in Moorfields. He dominated the Mission's work for over fifty years. The City Mission building in Russell Town Avenue was acquired for demolition in 1962.

Dean Lane. Russell Town Avenue was previously named Dean Lane. It was renamed in the mid-1920s to give the street a new image, but it failed. As one resident put it, 'It ain't in Russell Town and it ain't an' Avenue.' This scene was captured in 1918 after the war with Germany was over. It was indeed 'Peace at last.' Unfortunately, it only lasted until 1939.

Cattybrook Street, *c.* 1950. A superb photograph taken by Noreen Shaw (nee Fowler) who lived with her parents at No. 64. With Russell Town Avenue closed for some reason, buses were diverted along Cattybrook Street. On the left of the picture is the top of the signal box at Lawrence Hill station.

Cattybrook Street; the stretch from Russell Town Avenue to Jane Street. The firm of A.H. Pinnell, electric welders were on one side, plus nineteen houses (Nos. 47-65). George Lockier lived at the far end. Today this is the only house remaining, and is home to the same family. All the other houses were demolished in the late 1950s.

Dove Inn, Church Road, Redfield 1955. Another George's pub, on the corner of the then very narrow Dove Lane. This building still remains, although it has been much altered since it closed as a pub in the late 1960s.

The Shepherds Rest, No.8 Church Road. The alleyway to the right of this pub is Providence Place, which can still be seen today. Another path to the left, Clarence Place, led to Moorfields Square, now a children's play area. The pub was pulled down in 1964 and replaced by a tree and a piece of grass.

Ale and Porter Stores, on the other corner of Dove Lane and Church Road. Note the brick extension to the original. This large structure was part of a rank known as Moorfields Place. The pub always had attractive hanging baskets of flowers outside in the summer. It was acquired for demolition in 1962.

The London House in 1948. Russell Town Avenue, Nos. 51-52, on the corner of Procter Street. This was an off-licence, run in the 1930s by the Appletons. It was rebuilt as shown in 1936 along with eight houses in Proctor Street known as 'church tenements'. Proctor Street including the London House was demolished in 1962/63.

The Prince of Wales. An 'out door' beer retailer, not a pub but an off-licence. Situated on the corner of Cattybrook Street and Russell Town Avenue. On the opposite corner was a fish and chip shop. The Prince of Wales was demolished in 1959, as part of the redevelopment of Moorfields.

At number 39 Dean Street, several generations of the Carter family gathered in the back garden for this image, the grandparents having place of honour in the front.

Moorfields, Carlton Park, St George School. Perhaps best known as Carlton Park, this well-proportioned building was opened in 1900 as Moorfields Board School. An infants school was built off left, and a special school block off right. In the 1950s this was Carlton Park Secondary Modern Boy's School (headmaster Mr Greenland), which became part of St George Comprehensive in 1965. The new St George School was built next to this imposing block between 1967 and 1970.

Woodcock Shield. In 1946 Carlton Park School Football Team won the Woodcock Shield and the League Shield. The proud team are seen with both trophies. The teacher on the extreme right is Ivor 'Duke' Davies, who taught at Avonvale, Barton Hill and Carlton Park schools.

A Carlton Park School photograph, taken during the 1957/58 school year. The teacher is once again Mr Davies. He is probably the best-remembered teacher in the area and only died in the late 1990s.

The Hall at Carlton Park School. This was the hall of the main Carlton Park block situated on the first floor of the building. Reached by two flights of stairs, one at each end of the building, classrooms are off to the right. The structure is still used as part of St George Community School although the hall has recently been divided into classrooms.

David (one of the authors, sat down) and
John Stephenson on one of Carlton Park
School's vehicles in 1954. Overalls were
worn by the children to keep their own
clothes cleaner. They also had a sleep after
their meal break.

The May Festival. The University Settlement held their festival on Moorfields playing field
in 1928. This field had previously been the site of Brown's market gardens.

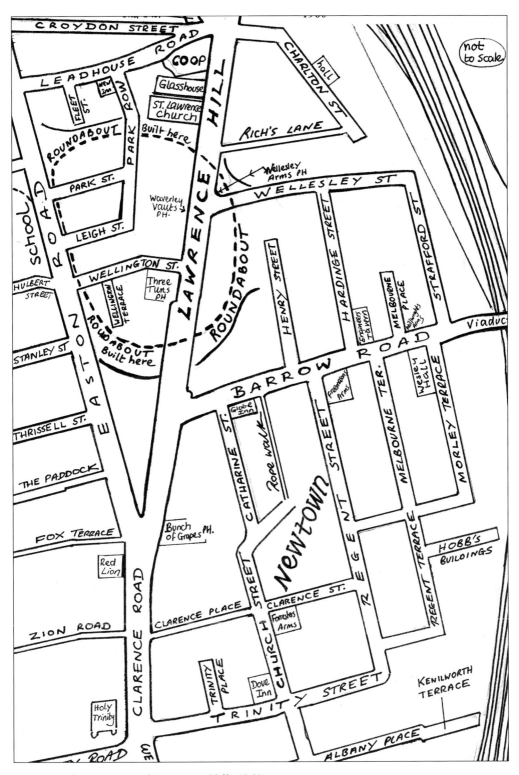

Key map of Newtown and Lawrence Hill, 1960.

# A Postscript From the Authors

**David Stepehenson**: 'As a young lad, I was supposed to get off the bus at Redfield, but I suffered from travel sickness so instead I usually got off in Old Market. I recall many grand buildings and a lot of 'dumps'. As a teenager I worked for a blind door to door salesman. We often visited these areas, most of them now gone. I was even allowed into the pubs, just like a guide dog. In 1969, I worked as a bus conductor, often at Lawrence Hill or Old Market. So much was changing; in the 1980s I began taking photographs'.

**Andy Jones:** Chairman of the Barton Hill History Group was born in the pivotal year of 1965: 'Walking to work via Lawrence Hill, Newtown and Old Market, I often wish I was doing the same route forty years ago. Luckily, many fine photographs have emerged, so it is just about possible to recreate that lost landscape – on a good day!

For me growing up, the area meant Max Williams. Countless Saturday afternoons were spent there in the 1970s. It was an amazing shop, crammed full of Dinky cars, Hornby trains and Airfix kits. It was 'Welcome to the Pleasure Dome'. Mrs Williams was always helpful and friendly when, after hours of deliberation I finally went to the counter with an Airfix Spitfire!'

The whole thing about the Lawrence Hill roundabout and what was there before is particularly fascinating to me because I was too young to remember the Lawrence Hill of 1967. I must have passed the Glass House on many occasions but was too young to care! On another level my dad always spoke in reverential terms about Brain's cycle shop and how he had got his first bike there in 1932. I can also recall my mother talking about cutting through Wellington Street or Leadhouse Road on her way to work at the now long-gone Newfoundland Road School.

For me growing up, the area meant Max Williams. Countless Saturday afternoons were spent there in the 1970s. It was an amazing shop, crammed full of Dinky cars, Hornby trains and Airfix kits. It was 'Welcome to the Pleasure Dome'. Mrs Williams was always helpful and friendly when, after hours of deliberation I finally went to the counter with an Airfix Spitfire!'

**Ernie Haste**: 'I have lived in Redfield all my life and in recent years have served on the Committee of the Barton Hill History Group. It has given me great pleasure helping to produce this book. I have seen many changes over the years in these areas. I am sorry to say not one for the betterment of the area. A prime example is the Lawrence Hill roundabout. Years ago it was a pleasure to walk from Redfield to Old Market and Castle Street; there were so many shops. I also recall queuing to see a film at the Kings, and then going to Owen's for a faggot and peas supper. Compared to those days Old Market today is dead. One of my hobbies has been photography, and many of my photos are included in this book'.

**David Cheesley**: 'Being a railway enthusiast, my best memories of the area covered by this book are bound to be railway-orientated – happy hours train-spotting on Lawrence Hill in the 1960s or on the bridge at Barrow Road. I didn't realise at the time that I was witnessing the last years of steam in Bristol. I watched the demolition of vast areas of Lawrence Hill and Easton and the whole of Newtown'.

If you would like to comment about this book or if you have photographs, documents, memories or newspaper cuttings, please write to:

David Stephenson
7 New Cheltenham Road
Kingswood
Bristol
BS15 1TH.

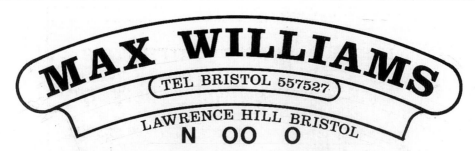